SEP   2008

J 978.00497 DE CAPUA
De Capua, Sarah
The Shawnee

2008/09/06

P9-CJZ-899

FIRST AMERICANS

The Shawnee

Alameda Free Library
1550 Oak Street
Alameda, CA 94501

SARAH De CAPUA

Marshall Cavendish
Benchmark
New York

ACKNOWLEDGMENTS

Series consultant: Raymond Bial

Marshall Cavendish Benchmark
99 White Plains Road
Tarrytown, New York 10591-9001
www.marshallcavendish.us

Text copyright © 2008 by Marshall Cavendish Corporation
Map and illustrations copyright © 2008 by Marshall Cavendish Corporation
Map by Rodica Prato
Craft illustrations by Chris Santoro

All rights reserved. No part of this book may be reproduced or utilized in any form or by any means electronic or mechanical, including photocopying, recording, or by any information storage and retrieval system, without permission from the copyright holders.
All Internet sites were available and accurate when sent to press.
The recipe on page 19 is from The Pumpkin Patch (http://www.pumpkin-patch.com/)

Library of Congress Cataloging-in-Publication Data
De Capua, Sarah.
   The Shawnee / Sarah De Capua.
       p. cm. — (First Americans)
   Summary: "Provides comprehensive information on the background, lifestyle,
beliefs, and present-day lives of the Shawnee people"—Provided by publisher.
   Includes bibliographical references and index.
   ISBN-13: 978-0-7614-2682-0
   1. Shawnee Indians—Juvenile literature. I. Title. II. Series.
   E99.S35D4 2007
   973.04'97317—dc22
2006034117

On the cover: A Shawnee boy in traditional dress at a powwow
Title page: Shawnee beaded leg bands

Photo Research by Connie Gardner
Cover photo by Nativestock.com: Marilyn Angel Wynn
Title page by Nativestock.com: Marilyn Angel Wynn
The photographs in this book are used by permission and through the courtesy of: Corbis: Kennan Ward, 4; Stefano Blanchetti, 18; David Muench, 26; Jon Davies/Jim Reed Photography, 31; Peter Turnley, 38. Nativestock.com: Marilyn Angel Wynn, 8, 9, 14, 22, 28, 29, 33, 34, 37. Granger Collection: 11, 13, 17. Raymond Bial: 23, 26.

Editor: Deborah Grahame
Publisher: Michelle Bisson
Editorial Director: Michelle Bisson
Art Director: Anahid Hamparian
Series designer: Symon Chow

Printed in China
1 3 5 6 4 2

CONTENTS

1 · WHO ARE THE SHAWNEE PEOPLE?

Members of the Shawnee [Shaw-NEE] Indian tribe live mostly in Oklahoma, Missouri, and Kansas beside their non-Indian neighbors. They do not live on reservations—separate areas of land—but they do have tribal headquarters. In all, there are about 15,000 Shawnee in the United States.

From the 1600s to the 1800s the Shawnee lived mainly in present-day Ohio and Kentucky, as well as in Tennessee's Cumberland River Valley. Their hunting grounds and villages stretched as far south as West Virginia, South Carolina, and Georgia. There were also Shawnee in Pennsylvania, and in Illinois and Indiana. This area, from the Atlantic coast to the Mississippi River and from South Carolina to Canada, was known as the Eastern Woodlands. It was a wilderness of thick forests, fertile soil, lush vegetation, and plentiful wildlife.

The Eastern Woodlands included what are known today as the Appalachian Mountains.

Streams, lakes, and rivers were full of fish. Deer and other game were present in great numbers and provided meat for the Shawnee. Nuts, berries, and plants were also available to eat. The Shawnee used wood and bark as building materials and fuel.

Many other tribes also lived in the Eastern Woodlands. They included tribes of the powerful Iroquois Confederacy, the Cherokee, the Delaware, and many others. The Shawnee were friendly with some of these groups. However, they were enemies of other groups, such as the Iroquois. In the 1660s the Iroquois drove the Shawnee out of Ohio. They returned around 1730.

The Shawnee moved in small bands, or groups made up of family members. They searched for better farming and hunting lands. They also moved to avoid danger from enemy tribes, especially the Iroquois. Because the Shawnee moved so often, no one is sure of the location of the first Shawnee settlements. However, it is known that by the

This map shows the territory of the Shawnee before they were moved west of the Mississippi River.

mid-1700s about three thousand Shawnee lived in villages in the Ohio River Valley. This area became the center of the Shawnee nation. It is believed that more Shawnee lived in one place during this time than at any other time in the tribe's history.

The Shawnee first encountered Europeans in the 1530s, when Spanish explorers and traders came in search of gold and

A Shawnee village in the Ohio River Valley.

silver. By the early 1700s European **missionaries** and settlers arrived. The French and the English began to compete with each other for trade with the Native Americans. During the French and Indian War (1754–1763) France and England fought for control of North America. The fighting extended from the English colonies on the Atlantic coast to the Ohio

Missionaries taught Christianity to the Shawnee and other Native Americans.

Valley and what is now the Midwest, and north into Canada. The Shawnee fought on the French side. When the British won the war in 1763, they controlled all of North America east of the Mississippi River. The Shawnee then had to defend themselves and their land against English colonists and the Iroquois, who had fought for the British during the war.

When the American Revolution began in 1775, the Shawnee fought for the British. The Shawnee believed a British victory would help stop the arrival of settlers in their territory. When the British were defeated in 1783, the United States controlled most of the eastern part of the country. After more battles with the settlers, the Shawnee moved west of the Ohio River.

As thousands of American pioneers loaded wagons and boats and moved westward, the Shawnee attacked their cabins and settlements. U.S. soldiers were sent to defend the frontier settlements.

Throughout the 1700s and 1800s the Shawnee allied with

other tribes to defend their lands from settlers and soldiers. Sometimes they were victorious, while other times they were defeated. In the Treaty of Fort Greenville of 1795, the Shawnee and other tribes sold 25,000 square miles (64,750 square kilometers) of land to the United States for more than $25,000 worth of goods. The area included most of what are now Ohio, Indiana, and Michigan. Settlers continued to pour into the region and many of the Shawnee had to move again—to what are now Missouri, Kansas, and Texas.

The Shawnee and other Native Americans sometimes arranged terms for treaties with British officials.

In 1830 the U.S. Congress passed the Indian Removal Act. The law ordered that all remaining eastern tribes had to move west of the Mississippi River. Most of the Shawnee who remained in Ohio and Indiana moved to Missouri, Kansas, and Oklahoma. Many Shawnee settled on reservations in Oklahoma, then known as Indian Territory, and became ranchers and farmers. However, they endured many hardships, especially when the U.S. Congress passed the Dawes Act in 1887. This law broke up the reservations, and many Shawnee lost their land. Their struggles continued, even after Congress granted U.S. citizenship to Native Americans in 1924.

Beginning in 1934 Congress began to pass laws to improve the lives of Native Americans, including the Shawnee. These laws included the right to establish their own tribal governments, to manage their own resources, and to speak their native languages. In 1936 the Oklahoma Indian Welfare Act permitted more tribes in Oklahoma to form governments and to receive federal assistance.

Tecumseh

Born in 1768, Tecumseh was a young Shawnee chief when he tried to unite Native American tribes against the U.S. government. He wanted to protect Shawnee lands from settlement. Tecumseh was a great orator, or speaker, and a brilliant leader. He visited nearly every tribe between the Great Lakes and Florida. Tecumseh's brother, Tenskwatawa, also traveled to villages to tell others about Tecumseh's plans to unite the Native Americans.

Tecumseh fought with the British against the Americans in the War of 1812 (1812–1814). In 1813 he was killed in battle. His death ended the effort to bring the tribes together.

Tecumseh (1768–1813)

2 · LIFE IN THE EASTERN WOODLANDS

The Shawnee lived in *wegiwas*, or lodges, made from tree poles covered with bark or animal skins. The lodges were usually clustered in settlements along lakes, rivers, or streams. Each village contained between twenty and a few hundred lodges. In summer the Shawnee lived in rectangular lodges with arched roofs, and in winter their lodges were circular with domed roofs. Sometimes the Shawnee built a log fence around the village to protect it from attacks by tribal enemies and, later, settlers or U.S. Army troops.

Each lodge had one large room where a family ate, cooked, slept, and prayed. There was a hole in the roof so that smoke from the cooking fire could escape. Lodges did not have windows. Doors were covered by animal skins or, after the arrival of European traders, blankets. The Shawnee slept on mats

Shawnee gardens consisted of corn, squash, beans, sweet potatoes, and other crops.

made from dried rushes—tall plants with hollow stems that grow in damp places, such as swamps. Sometimes they slept on animal skins or blankets.

Some villages also had a *msi-kah-me-kwi* (em-SEE-kaa-MEE-kwee), or council house. The council house was larger than the lodges and usually was located in the center of the village. It was used for ceremonies, meetings, and as protection during attacks.

The Shawnee were divided into five large groups or bands: the Kishpoko, the Chalaakaatha, the Thawikila, the Mekoche, and the Pekowi. Each group had its own responsibilities, such as carrying out warfare, addressing political issues, and taking care of tribal rituals. Each band had a peace chief and a war chief. The peace chief managed daily activities, and the war chief led warriors into battle. Chiefs could be men or women. Chiefs were sometimes chosen by **tribal councils**, but usually the son or daughter of a chief also became a chief.

Each Shawnee band was made up of many **clans**. Clan names included Snake, Turtle, Bear, Deer, Owl, and Wolf. Clans were named after animals because the Shawnee believed animal spirits protected them.

Shawnee families were made up of parents, children, grandparents, aunts, and uncles. Women planted and harvested the crops; gathered nuts, berries, roots, firewood, and bark;

A tribal council meets to discuss important issues.

and made clothing and tools. Men were the heads of families. They hunted, traded, and fought in battle. In spring, men cleared the fields, and the women and children planted corn, pumpkins, squash, sweet potatoes, beans, and tobacco.

The Shawnee fished with spears and nets. The men hunted deer, as the Shawnee depended on this animal for food and materials for clothing and other needs. They also hunted

Riding in a canoe was an effective way for some Native Americans to fish.

Pumpkin Corn Muffins

Pumpkin and corn were important crops to the Shawnee. These ingredients can be combined to make delicious pumpkin corn muffins. Ask an adult to help you make this recipe. Always wash your hands with soap and water before you begin.

$1\frac{1}{4}$ cups all-purpose flour
1 cup yellow corn meal
$\frac{1}{3}$ cup granulated sugar
4 teaspoons baking powder
$\frac{1}{2}$ teaspoon salt

2 large eggs
$1\frac{1}{4}$ cups pumpkin puree
$\frac{1}{3}$ cup milk
$\frac{1}{4}$ cup vegetable oil

Preheat oven to 375°F. Grease a twelve-muffin tin. (You can also line the tin with paper muffin cups.) Combine flour, corn meal, sugar, baking powder, and salt in a large bowl. Beat eggs, pumpkin, milk, and vegetable oil in a medium bowl until combined. Add to flour mixture. Mix thoroughly. Spoon batter into muffin cups until they are about three-quarters full. Bake for 25 to 30 minutes or until wooden toothpick inserted in the center comes out clean. Serve warm. Makes 12 muffins.

turkey, squirrel, rabbit, bear, raccoon, and moose. The Shawnee hunted on foot or on horseback. They used bows and arrows, stone knives, slingshots, or clubs as weapons. After the arrival of Europeans, they used guns that they obtained in trade or during battles.

Shawnee children learned their roles by watching and imitating the adults. Girls followed their mothers around the camp, helped with crops, went gathering in the woods, and learned to make clothes. Boys followed their fathers and learned to hunt, to clear fields, and to fight as warriors.

Shawnee boys and girls took part in a ritual called the **vision quest**. At about seven years old, boys and girls went off into the woods alone. There they would not eat or drink until their guardian spirit appeared to them. The Shawnee believed these spirit guides protected them throughout their lives.

Shawnee clothing was simple and well suited for life in the woodlands. Men wore leggings and **breechcloths**

Shawnee "Football"

Although the Shawnee were often busy around the village, children and adults liked to play sports and games. From ball games to footraces, the Shawnee enjoyed many leisure activities.

The Shawnee particularly enjoyed a game similar to modern football. Players used a ball made of animal skin stuffed with deer hair. It was smaller than today's footballs. Men and boys kicked the ball; they were not allowed to touch it with their hands. Women and girls could kick or carry the ball. Each team had a line at the end of a field that was about 100 yards (91 meters) long. The team who got the ball across the other team's line scored a point. Usually, it took only one point to win. It could take a long time to score because opposing players could push or shove each other, and they could **intercept** passes. They could also knock players on the ground and hold them there in an attempt to wrestle the ball away. It was a very rough game—even when the men and boys played against the women and girls.

made from animal skins. Women wore skirts, also sewn from animal skins. The Shawnee did not wear shirts until after the Europeans came, but they often wore animal-skin ponchos when the weather was cold. After the arrival of European traders, men and women sometimes wore leather clothing. Children wore the same kind of clothing as their parents. Men, women, and children also wore moccasins. Clothing and moccasins were sometimes decorated with feathers, beads, and dyed porcupine quills, or colored with animal or vegetable dyes.

Shawnee beaded moccasins.

Shawnee men and women wore their hair long, but men often shaved their heads before going into battle. Men wore headbands. They usually attached an owl, hawk, or eagle feather to the headbands. The Shawnee also wore unique headpieces called roach headdresses. These were made from deer or porcupine hair that was pushed through pieces of animal bone so that it stood straight up. Feathers were attached to the headdresses.

Shawnee men also wore jewelry. They wore chokers, necklaces, or nose rings made of shell or bone. After the arrival of Europeans, this jewelry, as well as bracelets and armbands, was made from glass beads or silver.

A Shawnee in traditional clothing, including a roach headdress.

Shawnee Beaded Necklace

The Shawnee are well known for their colorful beadwork on clothing, moccasins, and jewelry. You can make your own beaded necklace to share what you have learned about the Shawnee.

You will need:

- String, in the length you want your necklace to be.
- A small glass pendant in the shape of a turtle, or any of the other animal clan names mentioned in this book. The turtle used here is green, but you can find them in many colors at craft stores.
- An assortment of white, gold, and green round beads.
- An assortment of white-colored pipe beads.

Spread out newspaper to cover and protect your work area. String the turtle pendant to the halfway point of the length of string. At one side of the turtle pendant, string beads in the following order:

1 gold bead
5 white beads
3 green (or other color) beads
5 white beads
1 gold bead
1 pipe bead

Keep stringing beads in this order until you have finished one side of the necklace. Tie a knot at the end of the string to keep the beads in place. (Remember to leave enough string so you can tie it to the other end and put it around your neck.) Repeat beads on the other side of the pendant until the necklace is completely beaded. Tie a knot at the end of the string. Tie the two ends together, and your necklace is ready to wear!

3 · SHAWNEE BELIEFS

The Shawnee believed that nature was sacred. Everything on earth, including the ground, trees, water, rocks, and animals, had a spirit. Everything in the sky—the sun, moon, and stars—also had a spirit. The Shawnee danced, chanted, and prayed to these spirits to ask for their help in daily living and solving problems. The Shawnee believed spirits were responsible for health. Good spirits brought good health, while evil spirits brought sickness. Shawnee healers called **shamans** cared for the sick and wounded. Shamans used herbs, roots, prayers, and sacred objects to heal people.

Like other Native Americans, the Shawnee believed that the Great Spirit ruled over nature and the universe. The Shawnee also worshipped Our Grandmother as the creator of their people. Our Grandmother gave sacred bundles called

The Shawnee believed everything in nature had a spirit.

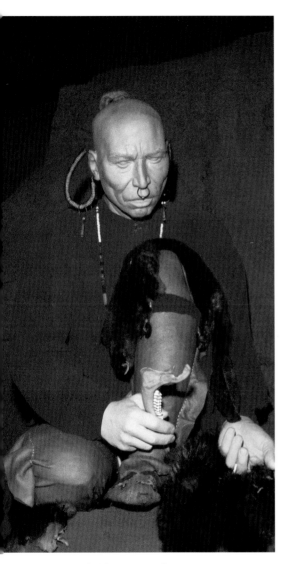
A Shawnee shaman.

meesawmi to her children, the Shawnee, to protect them from evil spirits. The *meesawmi* contained objects, such as bird feathers, animal bones, or tiny bone or wood carvings, that were believed to possess special powers.

The Shawnee held ceremonies and dances to thank the good spirits for their protection and help. During the spring Bread Dance, the Shawnee prayed for abundant crops. At the fall Bread Dance, the Shawnee gave thanks for the crops they harvested. They also asked for enough wildlife to hunt so they would have food to last through winter. The Green Corn Dance, held during the month of August, lasted as long as twelve days. During this festival, the Shawnee gave thanks for the corn harvest. At the same time, people who had done wrong to others or had broken tribal rules could ask their fellow villagers for forgiveness.

Marriages were important events among the Shawnee. Parents usually arranged, or at least approved, the marriages of their children. A young man's mother would speak to the mother of a young woman. The young man's mother would bring gifts, such as animal skins, to the woman's family. This was a way to show that the young man would be a good provider. If the young woman's family accepted the gifts, the couple would be promised to each other.

The Shawnee performed dances for many occasions.

The female members of the bride's family made a large feast, which was brought to the groom's home. The couple's family and friends attended the feast. Afterward, the couple was considered to be married.

When a baby was born, a naming ceremony was held ten days after the birth. In the days leading up to the ceremony, two elderly, well-respected men or women were asked to name the baby. They would pray to the Great Spirit for the right name. Each of them would suggest a name. The baby's parents picked one. The parents announced the baby's name during the feast for friends and relatives held at the naming ceremony.

At about three or four years old, Shawnee children experienced the Green Snake Ceremony. During the ceremony, the head of a green snake was placed briefly inside a child's mouth. The Shawnee believed this brought the child good luck and a long life.

Some Shawnee changed their names throughout their lives. This might occur if a person had a history of bad health,

How the Shawnee Came to Be

Our Grandmother, *Kohkumthena*, made the Shawnee. She taught them how to live good lives and how to work hard. When she was finished teaching the Shawnee, Our Grandmother went up to  her home in the sky. To this day, she sits there and watches her earth children from a window while she weaves a basket. When the basket is finished, she will gather up the Shawnee people in it and take them to live with her in the sky.

Our Grandmother has not yet returned to collect her children because she has not finished weaving the basket. Every night while she is sleeping, her grandson and her little dog undo the weaving she completed during the day. Someday, Our Grandmother will finish the basket. Then she will take her children to live with her.

or if a man was a poor hunter, or was often wounded in battle. It was hoped that the name change would improve the person's luck.

When a person died, the Shawnee held a special ceremony. The body was dressed in the person's finest clothing. Friends dug the grave, carried the body to it, and placed it inside. At the gravesite, friends and family members tossed bits of tobacco onto the body and prayed for the person's soul as it traveled to the afterworld. Shawnee were buried facing west, toward the setting sun. After the grave was filled back up with dirt, the person's family gave away his or her belongings to friends.

After the burial, a feast was held. Villagers observed a mourning period of twelve days. During the next year, the dead person's spouse wore the same clothing every day. Husbands did not wear jewelry. If the person who died was a well-respected member of the village, a feast was held one year after his or her death.

After trading with settlers began, the Shawnee wrapped their dead in wool blankets as part of the funeral preparations, while tribal members mourned their loss.

4 · A CHANGING WORLD

Today, the Shawnee live throughout the United States, but most live in Oklahoma or Ohio. There are three groups of Shawnee in Oklahoma: the Absentee Shawnee Tribe, the Eastern Shawnee Tribe, and the Loyal (or Cherokee) Shawnee Tribe. There are about 14,000 members of these three tribes. They do not live on reservations, but most live near their tribal headquarters. In Ohio, there are about six hundred members of the Shawnee Nation United Remnant Band (URB). Like the Oklahoma Shawnee, they do not have a reservation. However, they do own about 330 acres (134 hectares) in Shawandasse, which they use as a gathering place for traditional ceremonies and meetings.

The Shawnee have independent tribal governments made up of elected officials. All of the tribes have business councils,

A modern-day Shawnee council meeting.

which make decisions on matters that affect the entire tribe. Both men and women serve on the councils.

The Shawnee live in modern homes and work in many occupations, such as farmers, ranchers, teachers, lawyers, artists, doctors, and more. Children attend tribal schools or go to nearby public and private schools. Those who go on to colleges or universities do so at state or private institutions.

The Absentee Shawnee tribal headquarters are located in Shawnee, Oklahoma. There they maintain businesses, stores,

These children are members of the Shawnee Nation United Remnant Band in Ohio.

a museum, a restaurant, and a casino. The Absentee Shawnee are led by a five-member executive committee, which includes a governor.

The tribal headquarters of the Eastern Shawnee are located in West Seneca, Oklahoma. They, too, maintain businesses and stores, as well as a library and **powwow** grounds. They also operate a casino and travel center in nearby Seneca, Missouri. The Eastern Shawnee are led by a chief and a governing council.

Shawnee play a drum made of traditional materials.

Shawnee traditional costume.

The Loyal Shawnee Tribe has its headquarters in Miami, Oklahoma. The U.S. government recognizes the tribe through the Cherokee Indian Nation. In addition to businesses and stores, together with the Cherokee, the Loyal Shawnee operate a tribal heritage center and village where visitors can learn about Native American life. The Loyal Shawnee are led by a chairman. In 2001 they were granted separate recognition from the Cherokee by the U.S. government.

Members of the URB are **descendants** of the Shawnee who avoided removal to the reservations during the 1830s. The U.S. government and the Oklahoma Shawnee do not recognize the URB as an independent Shawnee tribe. However, the state of Ohio does recognize the tribe. On its lands in Shawandasse, the URB

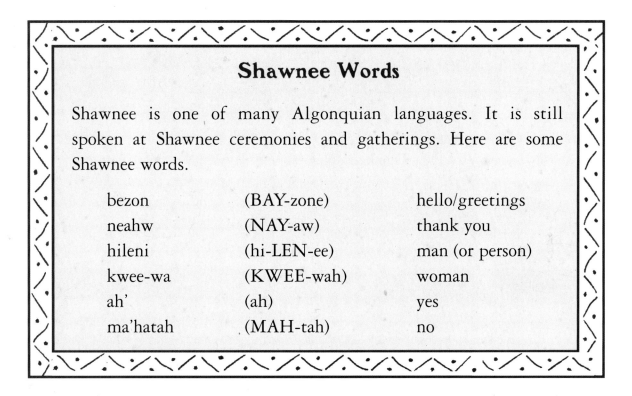

Shawnee Words

Shawnee is one of many Algonquian languages. It is still spoken at Shawnee ceremonies and gatherings. Here are some Shawnee words.

bezon	(BAY-zone)	hello/greetings
neahw	(NAY-aw)	thank you
hileni	(hi-LEN-ee)	man (or person)
kwee-wa	(KWEE-wah)	woman
ah'	(ah)	yes
ma'hatah	(MAH-tah)	no

maintains a family campground and recreation area, which includes the Shawnee and Native American Woodland Museum. There are also family homes in Shawandasse.

While living successfully in the modern world, the Shawnee seek to educate their young people in the traditional ceremonies, songs, dances, crafts, and skills. This helps them keep their rich culture alive for future generations.

• TIME LINE

Before 1500	1530s	1670s	1754-1763	1768	1775-1783	1795
The Shawnee live as farmers and hunters in the Eastern Woodlands of the present-day United States.	The Shawnee encounter Spanish explorers.	The Shawnee encounter French and English explorers and traders.	The Shawnee fight alongside the French against the British during the French and Indian War.	Tecumseh is born in present-day Ohio.	The Shawnee fight with the British against the colonists in the American Revolution.	The Shawnee sell 25,000 square miles (64,750 square hectares) of land to the U.S. government.

Tecumseh is killed in battle.

Congress passes the Indian Removal Act.

Congress passes the Dawes Act.

Congress passes the Indian Citizenship Act, making all Native Americans U.S. citizens.

Congress passes the Indian Reorganization Act, recognizing the right of Native American tribes to form their own governments and manage their own resources.

Oklahoma Indian Welfare Act extends the 1934 act by permitting more tribes in Oklahoma to establish tribal governments and to receive financial help from the U.S. government.

The state of Ohio officially recognizes the Shawnee Nation United Remnant Band (URB). The URB begins buying back tribal lands in central Ohio.

1813   1830   1887   1924   1934   1936   1980

GLOSSARY

breechcloths: Simple men's cloth or skin garments worn between the legs and around the waist.

clans: Groups of families who are related to each other.

descendants: The children, grandchildren, and so on of a person who lived long ago.

intercept: To stop the movement of someone or something.

missionaries: People sent by a church or a religious group to convert native people to Christianity.

powwow: A Native American social gathering that includes traditional dances.

shamans: Native American healers who cured the sick and acted as links between the spirit world and humans.

tribal councils: Groups of leaders who hold meetings to discuss important issues and make decisions about them.

vision quest: A rite of passage in which a Native American youth journeys alone into the wilderness to seek spiritual guidance and direction.

FIND OUT MORE

Books

Fitterer, C. Ann. *Tecumseh: Chief of the Shawnee*. Chanhassen, MN: The Child's World, 2002.

Koestler-Grack, Rachel A. *Tecumseh: 1768–1813*. Mankato, MN: Blue Earth Books, 2003.

Mattern, Joanne. *The Shawnee Indians*. Mankato, MN: Capstone Press, 2001.

Webster, M. L. *On the Trail Made of Dawn: Native American Creation Stories*. North Haven, CT: Linnet Books, 2001.

Yacowitz, Caryn. *Shawnee Indians*. Chicago: Heinemann, 2003.

Web Sites

Absentee Shawnee Tribe

www.astribe.com

This is the official Web site of the Absentee Shawnee Tribe. Here you'll find information about tribal government, businesses, and more.

Shawnee Tribe of Oklahoma

www.easternshawnee.org

This is the official Web site of the Eastern Shawnee. You can learn about the annual powwow, how the business council works, the history of the Eastern Shawnee, and current tribal news.

Indians.org

www.indians.org

This site provides information on the history and culture of the Shawnee and other Native American tribes.

National Museum of the American Indian

www.nmai.si.edu

The National Museum of the American Indian is part of the Smithsonian Institution. Here you can view the museum's exhibits of Native American art, crafts, and more.

About the Author

Sarah De Capua is the author of many books, including biographies and geographical and historical titles. She has always been fascinated by the earliest inhabitants of North America. In the First Americans series, De Capua has also written *The Cherokee*, *The Cheyenne*, *The Comanche*, *The Iroquois*, and *The Shoshone*. Born and raised in Connecticut, she now resides in Colorado.

ALAMEDA FREE LIBRARY

INDEX

Page numbers in **boldface** are illustrations.